TUDOR AND STUART TIMES

Contents

TUDOR RULERS
The White Rose and the Red Rose — 2
Henry VIII and his court — 4
The break with Rome — 6
Queen Elizabeth I — 8
Armada! — 10

STUART RULERS
Roman Catholic plots — 12
Charles I and the Civil War — 14
The Second Civil War — 16
Oliver Cromwell — 18
Charles II — 20

TUDOR AND STUART FAMILY TREE — 22

LIFE IN TUDOR AND STUART TIMES
Life in the country — 24
Great Tudor and Stuart houses — 26
Life in the towns — 28
Trade and travel — 30
The loss of the *Mary Rose* — 32
Shakespeare and the Globe — 34
Adventurers – Sir Francis Drake — 36
Adventurers – Sir Walter Raleigh — 38
Plague! — 40
The Great Fire of London — 42
Science — 44
Religion and superstition — 46

Glossary and Index — 48

TUDOR RULERS

The White Rose and the Red Rose

On the 22nd August, 1485, two great armies met at Bosworth Field in Leicestershire. One army was led by the king of England, Richard III. The other army was led by a nobleman called Henry Tudor.

This was the last battle in what we call the 'Wars of the Roses'. Henry won the battle and killed Richard. Henry VII became the new king of England. He was the first Tudor ruler. (You can see the Tudor family tree on page 22.)

Many people, especially the Yorkists, did not think Henry should be king. Henry did not want civil war to break out again. The Wars of the Roses had weakened the country. He knew peace was needed for people to work at their trades and sell goods abroad.

By the end of Henry's reign England was a stronger country and the Tudor family's rule was safe. When Henry died his son, Henry VIII, did not have to fight a battle to become king.

King Richard III was head of the Yorkist family. Their symbol was the white rose.

Henry Tudor was head of the Lancastrian family. Their symbol was the red rose.

LOOKING AT EVIDENCE

There are many portraits and statues that tell us a lot about the Tudor rulers. We also have many letters and books written in Tudor times. However, historians have to be careful with this evidence because sometimes it does not tell us the whole truth.

▶ A medallion to celebrate the marriage of Henry VII and Elizabeth of York.

Henry was a man of lean and spare body, but very strong, somewhat taller than the average sort of men, of a wonderful beauty and fair complexion, of a merry smiling countenance, especially in conversation, his eyes grey, his teeth single, his hair thin, in all things quick and prompt wit, of a pricely stomach and high courage.

▲ This is a portrait of Richard III painted around 1520. You can see he has a hump on one shoulder. The hump was added to the painting years later by a different artist.

◀ This is what a friend of Henry VII wrote about him.

▲ Terracotta bust of Henry VII.

What did Henry VII do?

These are some of the things that Henry did during his rule. Can you think why?

- He married Elizabeth, who was a member of the Yorkist family.

- He started the Royal Navy to protect the shores of England, but he did not join in any wars abroad.

- He <u>taxed</u> his barons and stopped them having their own private armies to defend their castles.

Henry VIII and his court

Henry VIII became king when he was 18 years old. He was tall and strong, and wore expensive and colourful clothes. He encouraged his courtiers to do the same. He spoke several foreign languages, was interested in art, and could write music and play many instruments. He was also good at sports like jousting, hunting and tennis.

Henry owned many palaces and often moved his court, including courtiers and furniture, from one palace to another. His favourite palaces were at Greenwich, where he was born, and Hampton Court. Many foreign ambassadors were invited to his court. They wrote about their visits, often praising Henry.

▲ Henry invited a famous German painter called Hans Holbein to his court. This is one of many paintings of Henry VIII by Holbein. He always made Henry look strong, powerful and wise.

It is the prettiest thing in the world to see him play, his fair skin glowing through a shirt of the finest texture.

4

Henry's six wives

Henry desperately wanted to marry and have a son who could be king after he died. But Henry was not a patient man. Although he married six wives Henry only had one son, Edward.

When Henry died, Edward VI became king. But he was only nine years old and suffered from poor health. He ruled for six years and died when he was just fifteen.

1 Catherine of Aragon
Catherine was a Spanish princess. She had been married to Henry's older brother Arthur, who died suddenly. She was a popular queen. Catherine gave birth to four sons, but they all died. Only her daughter, Mary, survived. Henry wanted to end his marriage with Catherine so that he could marry again and have a son. He wanted to marry Anne Boleyn. To do this he had to ask the Pope's permission. The Pope refused, but Henry divorced Catherine anyway.

2 ▼ Anne Boleyn
Anne also had a daughter, but no son. Henry grew angry with her. He wanted to marry her lady-in-waiting, Jane Seymour. Anne was charged with treason and witchcraft, and was executed.

4 ▶ Anne of Cleves
Henry was advised to make friends with Germany. He sent Holbein to Germany to paint the portrait of a German princess called Anne of Cleves. Henry saw this portrait and decided to marry her. But when she came to England Henry thought she was ugly, and Anne disliked him. The King decided to divorce her at once.

5 Catherine Howard
In the very same year Henry married Catherine Howard, who was only 19 years old. By now Henry was 49 years old. Catherine made friends with younger courtiers. Henry became jealous when he found out she had boyfriends and had her executed.

3 ▶ Jane Seymour
Jane married Henry and had one son, but she died in childbirth. Their son was called Edward.

6 Catherine Parr
By the time Henry married his last wife, Catherine Parr, he was suffering from many illnesses. Catherine took care of Henry until his death in 1547.

The break with Rome

Like his father, Henry VIII was a keen Roman Catholic. He disliked the new Protestant religion which many people were supporting. He even wrote a book in Latin in support of the Roman Catholic Church. The Pope was so pleased with Henry that he named him 'Defender of the Faith'. But Henry's need for a son was soon to end his friendship with the Pope.

Henry thought that his wife, Catherine of Aragon, was not going to have a son, so he decided to divorce her. He wanted to marry Anne Boleyn, who was a Protestant. Henry needed permission from the Pope to divorce Catherine. He asked his chief advisor, Cardinal Wolsey, to persuade the Pope to annul his marriage to Catherine. But the Pope refused.

- Roman Catholics are Christians who believe that the leader of their Church is the Pope, who lives in Rome.

- Protestants are Christians who have different Church leaders and do not obey the Pope. They have simpler churches and services than the Roman Catholics, without gold ornaments and decorations.

Henry decided to disobey the Pope. He sacked Wolsey and divorced Catherine. He then decided to make himself head of the English Church, instead of the Pope. In 1534 Henry's Parliament made a new law called the 'Act of Supremacy'. Although Henry was still a Catholic this law meant he no longer had to obey the Pope.

▶ Hatfield House in Hertfordshire had belonged to the Bishop of Ely. After the Act of Supremacy, Henry made it one of his royal houses.

The dissolution of the monasteries

Now that Henry was head of the English Church he decided to make some changes. At that time all bibles were written in Latin, which only well-educated people like the clergy could read. Henry ordered the Bible to be translated into English and copies chained to church pulpits where ordinary people could hear them being read (but not steal them).

At that time people in England had to pay taxes to the Catholic Church. The wealthy monasteries were full of gold ornaments and valuable books. The monks and nuns in these monasteries still believed the Pope was their leader.

Henry decided to close and 'dissolve' the monasteries. He seized their wealth and lands for himself. Some church buildings became royal houses, others were given or sold to his courtiers.

▼ The dissolution of the monasteries made Henry VIII very rich. Many monasteries, like Fountains Abbey in Yorkshire, fell into ruin.

Queen Elizabeth I

Elizabeth comes to the throne

After the death of Henry VIII, his son Edward VI ruled for six years. When Edward died his half-sister Mary became queen. Mary I reigned for only five years and was very unpopular with Protestants because she wanted to make England a Catholic country again. She executed so many people that she became known as 'Bloody Mary'. After her death Henry's third child, Elizabeth, was crowned.

Henry VIII need not have worried about having a son to rule the kingdom. His daughter Elizabeth became the most popular and famous Tudor monarch of them all!

▶ This painting of Elizabeth shows her as a powerful ruler, standing on the world.

▲ Queen Elizabeth dancing at Penshurst Place.

Elizabeth and her Court

Elizabeth I was very well-educated. She could read Latin and Greek and spoke several languages. This meant that she could speak to foreign ambassadors in their own language. She invited many ambassadors and scholars to her court. She entertained them with music, plays, jousting, dancing and the reading of poetry. She encouraged her courtiers to be good musicians and actors. She wore fine dresses with jewels sewn on. She was the first person to wear silk stockings.

8

Progresses and palaces

Elizabeth never married, although many people wanted to marry her. She spent most of her time moving, or 'progressing', from one of her palaces to another, followed by all her servants and courtiers.

Elizabeth also invited herself to the great homes of her rich courtiers. Many of them had to make their homes even bigger to make room for all Elizabeth's servants. This was so expensive that some of her courtiers nearly went bankrupt. By continually moving, Elizabeth made her rich nobles pay for her court.

I am already bound unto a husband, which is the Kingdom of England.

▼ Elizabeth travelled around the south-east of England on horseback or in a litter. Ordinary people could see their queen for themselves on these journeys. Elizabeth became very popular.

Armada!

The Spanish enemy

Elizabeth I and the King of Spain, Philip II, were enemies. Elizabeth had annoyed Philip by refusing his offer of marriage. Philip believed that the Pope wanted him to invade England and make it Roman Catholic again. In 1587 Philip began to prepare for this invasion. He had many warships called galleons built in Spanish and Portuguese ports.

An English sailor called Francis Drake slowed down these preparations. He organized an attack which destroyed many of the ships built in the Spanish harbour of Cadiz.

I have singed the King of Spain's beard.

The Course of the Spanish Armada

29th July Armada first sighted by an English ship.

31st July Battle of Plymouth.

1st August Battle of Portland Bill.

3rd and 4th August Battles at the Isle of Wight.

7th and 8th August English fireships are launched.

8th August Battle of Gravelines.

Land's End • Plymouth • Weymouth • Portsmouth • Isle of Wight • London • Dover • Calais

▲ Painting of the defeat of the Spanish Armada.

The Armada sails

By 1588 Philip II's armada of ships was ready to sail. The Armada sailed up the English Channel and along the south coast in order to frighten and attack English ships. As the Armada was spotted the English lit beacon fires along the coast to warn others of the danger. The Armada reached the French port of Calais and prepared to invade England.

Francis Drake sailed in secret from England taking eight old English ships with him. He set fire to these ships and let the wind blow them into Calais harbour. The Spaniards were frightened that their galleons would catch fire. They sailed out of the harbour in panic. The English warships were waiting for them. They attacked and defeated the Spaniards at the Battle of Gravelines. When they returned to Tilbury harbour Elizabeth herself was there to praise them.

I have the body of a weak and feeble woman, but I have the heart and stomach of a king, and a king of England too, and I think foul scorn of that Parma and Spain, and any Prince of Europe, should dare to invade the borders of my realm.

The remaining ships of the Armada sailed north to Scotland and Ireland. Many ships were wrecked in storms. Spanish sailors drowned or died of disease. Others were killed when they reached Ireland.

STUART RULERS

Roman Catholic plots

Mary Queen of Scots

Elizabeth I liked the Protestants and was afraid of the Roman Catholics. She stopped Roman Catholics worshipping and took away a lot of their lands.

Scotland was ruled by Mary I, who was a Roman Catholic. Mary plotted with her supporters to kill Elizabeth and become queen of England. Elizabeth discovered the plot and, in 1587, had Mary executed. Mary's son James became the new king of Scotland.

James I is crowned

In 1603 Queen Elizabeth I died. James was her nearest relative. He rode to London and was crowned James I of England, the first of the Stuart kings.

James I did not hate the Roman Catholics. He wanted to let them worship freely and give them their lands back. But members of Parliament were keen Protestants. They persuaded James to take even more money and land away from the Roman Catholics.

The Gunpowder Plot

A Roman Catholic nobleman called Robert Catesby and seven other Roman Catholics decided to kill King James. They planned to blow up the King and all his ministers when they opened Parliament on November 5th, 1605. After the explosion they planned a Roman Catholic <u>rebellion</u> all over the country. One of the plotters was called Guy Fawkes. He was an expert in the use of gunpowder. It was Guy Fawkes' job to light the gunpowder.

1 ▲ The plotters rented a cellar underneath the House of Lords. They filled it with 36 barrels of gunpowder. One of the plotters had a friend in the House of Lords called Lord Mounteagle. He sent a letter to Lord Mounteagle to warn him not to go to the opening of Parliament. King James' men found the letter. But the letter did not name the plotters or tell them about the gunpowder.

2 ▲ Guy Fawkes went to the House of Lords to light the fuse. He was carrying a watch, a lantern and a tinder box. Soldiers saw him. They guessed what he was doing.

3 ▲ Guy Fawkes was taken to the Tower of London. He was tortured on the rack until he named the other plotters.

4 ◀ Guy Fawkes and most of the plotters were taken into the middle of London. A great crowd gathered to watch the plotters being hanged, drawn and quartered.

Charles I and the Civil War

King James I died in 1625. His son, Charles, became king of England. Charles I soon began to quarrel with members of Parliament. They were annoyed at all the money Charles was spending on a war with Spain. In 1629 Charles decided to close Parliament and rule the country himself. He taxed rich people and put many of his enemies in prison in the Tower of London.

In 1637 Charles tried to make the Scots worship in the same way as the English. The Scots refused to worship in this way and sent an army into England. Charles needed money to fight the Scots. In 1640 he recalled members to Parliament and asked them to raise the money, but many refused. Charles tried to arrest the leaders, but they escaped.

The members of Parliament decided to fight the King. They began to raise an army. Charles left London and also began to raise an army. Most people in London supported Parliament. Civil war had begun!

Cavaliers wore leather coats and iron breast plates. They fought with pistols and swords.

▲ **Charles I was unpopular, especially with the ordinary people of London.**

Pikesmen wore iron helmets and armour.

The main battle sites of the Civil War.

Soldiers wore leather jackets to protect them, and belts with wooden bottles of gunpowder and bags of bullets.

Cavaliers and Roundheads

People who supported Charles were called Royalists or 'Cavaliers'. 'Cavalier' means 'horseman'. Those who supported Parliament were called 'Roundheads', because they had short haircuts.

Many people did not want there to be a war. Families argued over which side to join. Some fathers ended up fighting their own sons in battle.

The First Civil War

At first the Cavaliers seemed to be winning. In 1642 the Cavaliers and Roundheads met at the Battle of Edgehill. The Roundheads were defeated. Charles moved his headquarters to Oxford.

One member of Parliament, Oliver Cromwell, decided that the Roundheads needed a better army. He gave his soldiers proper training, uniforms, and a regular wage. He called them the 'New Model Army'.

In 1644 the Scots joined forces with Parliament's side. At the Battle of Marston Moor the New Model Army and the Scots defeated a Royalist army. At the Battle of Naseby the remaining Royalists were defeated, but Charles I refused to surrender.

Both armies had many foot soldiers who fought with pikes and muskets.

The Second Civil War

After the Battle of Naseby Charles I fled to Scotland. But the Scots sold Charles back to Parliament.

Parliament and the New Model Army could not agree what to do with the King. Charles escaped from Hampton Court and fled to Carisbrooke Castle, on the Isle of Wight.

Charles planned to ask the Scots to change sides and help him. But the governor of Carisbrooke Castle refused to help Charles plot against Parliament. He handed Charles back to Parliament.

The Scots did send an army into England to help Charles. Many Royalists joined them. Oliver Cromwell met this large army with his smaller New Model Army. At the Battle of Preston Bridge the Scots and Royalists were defeated again.

The Scots and Royalists were no match for the well trained New Model Army soldiers.

◀ A 17th century drawing of the execution of Charles I.

There was such a groan by the thousands there present, as I never heard before and desire I may never hear again.

The execution of Charles I

Parliament tried Charles in front of a court of members of Parliament. Charles said that because he was the king no one could try him. He even refused to take off his hat in court. The court found him guilty of treason and sentenced him to death.

In 1649 Charles stood outside his own Banqueting Hall in London before a large crowd. He said a last goodbye to his children. He placed his head on the block. When the executioner's axe came down there was a great groan from the crowd. The executioner then held up the King's head for everyone to see.

◀ The warrant for Charles I's execution was signed by the 59 men who tried him. Cromwell's signature is the third one down on the left.

17

Oliver Cromwell

The death of King Charles I angered Royalists and Roman Catholics all over Europe. Royalists and Roman Catholics in Ireland formed an army to fight Cromwell and Parliament. They wanted to make Charles I's son (who was also called Charles) the new king. Many Scots also wanted Charles to be the new king.

▲ This is a portrait of Cromwell by Samuel Cooper. Cromwell told Cooper to paint him "warts and all".

Cromwell took the New Model Army to Ireland in 1649 and defeated the Irish. Then he went to Scotland and defeated the Scottish Royalists at the Battle of Dunbar. In 1651 he defeated another Scottish and English Royalist army at the Battle of Worcester.

Charles I's son fled from the Roundhead soldiers. Once he had to hide in an old oak tree. Another time he had to disguise himself as a farmer. Finally he escaped to Normandy.

Lord Protector of England

Now that the Royalists had been defeated, Parliament and the New Model Army ruled England. But they could not agree on how to govern the country. Cromwell thought England needed a strong leader. In 1653 he went to London and closed Parliament. Cromwell was made 'Lord Protector' and ruled the country himself.

Cromwell was a Puritan. He tried to make everyone live like the Puritans. He made laws to stop people dancing, gambling, horse racing or going to the theatre. He tried to make people worship in the simple Puritan way. Many people hated these new laws.

When Cromwell died in 1658, his son Richard became Lord Protector. But Richard did not like ruling and resigned. The Army wanted a strong leader to rule the country. They invited Charles I's son to return to England and become King Charles II.

▲ This picture shows Oliver Cromwell closing Parliament and sending the members away.

The New Model Army

The New Model Army was the best army in the country at that time. The soldiers all believed in the same religion. They were Puritans. They were very well trained and disciplined. They had better muskets, wore uniforms and were paid more than other soldiers.

▲ This 17th century coin shows a picture of Oliver Cromwell.

Charles II

Publick matters in a most sad condition; seamen discouraged for want of pay, and are not to be governed; as matters are now, can any fleete go out next year. Our enemies, French and Dutch, and grow more by our poverty

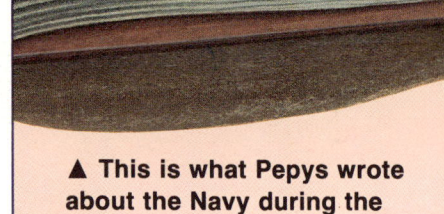

▲ **This is what Pepys wrote about the Navy during the reign of Charles II.**

◀ A 17th century oil painting of Charles II.

The Restoration

In 1660 Charles returned to England and was crowned Charles II. This time is called 'The Restoration' because the monarchy was 'restored'. Many people were glad that the King was back.

The new King was very popular. He dressed in rich clothes and loved parties. He forgave many of his father's old enemies and 'restored' Parliament. He let people enjoy all the things the Puritans had stopped, like gambling and horse racing. The King also supported new ideas about science, mathematics and navigation (see pages 44/45).

Pepys' Diary

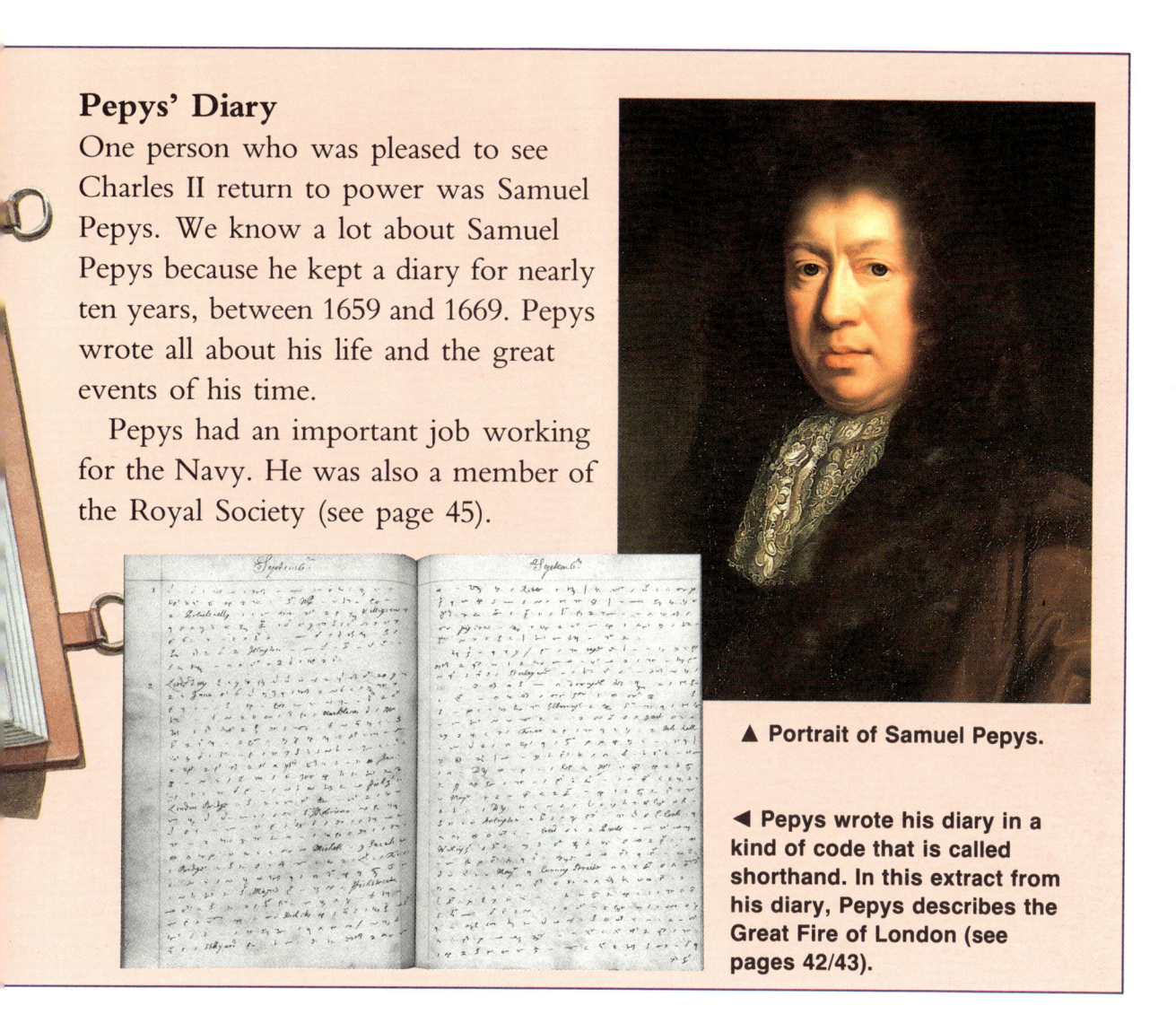

One person who was pleased to see Charles II return to power was Samuel Pepys. We know a lot about Samuel Pepys because he kept a diary for nearly ten years, between 1659 and 1669. Pepys wrote all about his life and the great events of his time.

Pepys had an important job working for the Navy. He was also a member of the Royal Society (see page 45).

▲ Portrait of Samuel Pepys.

◄ Pepys wrote his diary in a kind of code that is called shorthand. In this extract from his diary, Pepys describes the Great Fire of London (see pages 42/43).

Power to the Parliament

But things soon began to go wrong. Charles II began to rule more like Charles I had done. When Parliament refused to give Charles money to fight the Dutch, Charles closed Parliament. Charles died in 1685, leaving no children and an unhappy country.

After the death of Charles, his brother James became king. King James II also became unpopular and, in 1688, he resigned as king.

Most English people were tired of being ordered about and being taxed. They wanted a monarch, but they also wanted Parliament to stop that monarch having too much power. So, in 1689, Parliament invited a Dutch Protestant ruler to be king of England. Although William III became king, the real power to rule the country and make laws was held by Parliament. Parliament still rules our country today.

Tudor and Stuart Family Tree

Arthur

Margaret m. James IV of Scotland

Henry VIII m. 1. Catherine of Aragon
                2. Anne Boleyn
                3. Jane Seymour
                4. Anne of Cleves
                5. Catherine Howard
                6. Catherine Parr

Mary I m. Philip II of Spain

James V of Scotland

Mary, Queen of Scots m. Lord Darnley

James I m. Anne of Denmark

Henry

Charles II

Henry VII m. Elizabeth of York

Elizabeth   Mary

Elizabeth I   Edward VI

Charles I m. Henrietta Maria   Elizabeth

Mary m. William of Orange   James II

William III   Mary II   Anne

Everyday life in Tudor and Stuart Times

Life in the country

Working on the land

In Tudor and Stuart times most people lived in small villages in the country. Most villages had a miller, blacksmith, baker, shoemaker and wheelwright. Most people were farmers. Farmers worked hard all the year round. In the autumn they sowed their strips of land with seed and beat the ground with flails to spread the seed evenly. In the winter they <u>threshed</u> corn in sheds, cut hedges and spread dung on the soil. They ploughed up fields that had been left to grow grass. In the spring they planted their crops. In the summer they collected the hay and washed and sheared sheep to sell the wool.

Village houses

Poor people lived in simple cottages with thatched roofs and earthen floors. The whole family lived in one small room with a bed and straw mattress behind a curtain at the end of the room. Furniture was very simple. Wealthier farmers had houses built mostly from wood, called 'half-timbered', with two or more rooms. Rich landowners and merchants lived in manor houses.

◀ Painting showing 16th century farmers shearing their sheep.

Church and holydays

The parish church was the centre of life in the village. It was often the only building made of stone, with a tower or spire to house a large bell. The bell was rung on important days and to warn the villagers of danger. (Bells were rung in 1588 to warn people of the approach of the Spanish Armada.) The parson knew all the villagers. He conducted weddings, funerals and baptisms. He often acted as schoolmaster and lawyer because he was one of the few people who could read and write.

Everyone had to go to church on a Sunday or they had to pay a fine. After church and on special holydays the villagers had time for morris dancing, wrestling, bowls and cockfighting. They also played football, but there were no proper rules or referees. Many players were hurt in fights. During Stuart times violent games were stopped by King James I, and later by the followers of Oliver Cromwell.

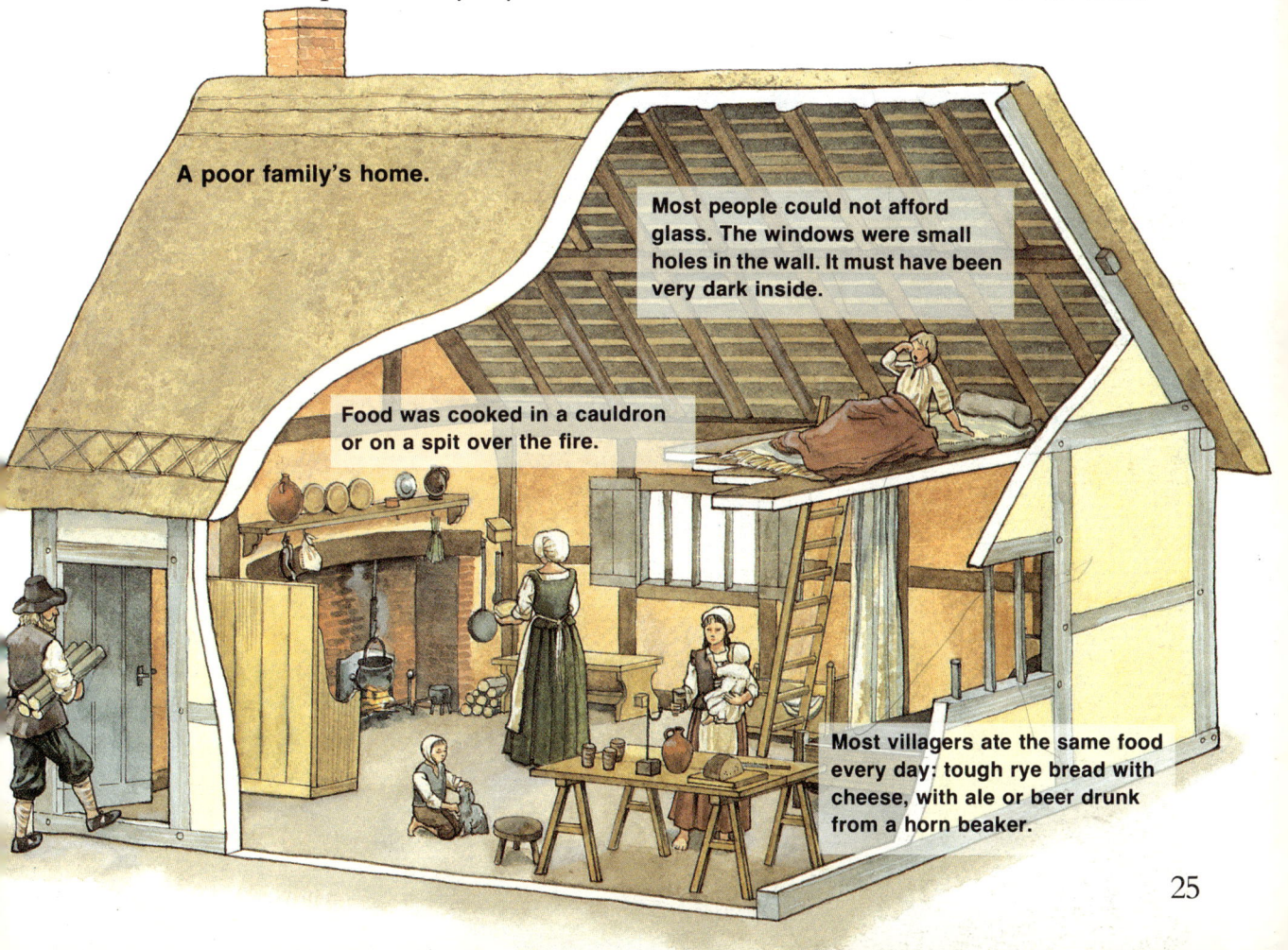

As concerning football I protest unto you that it may rather be called a friendlie kind of fight rather than a play or recreation - a bloody and murdering practice than a fellow pastime sport.

A poor family's home.

Most people could not afford glass. The windows were small holes in the wall. It must have been very dark inside.

Food was cooked in a cauldron or on a spit over the fire.

Most villagers ate the same food every day: tough rye bread with cheese, with ale or beer drunk from a horn beaker.

25

Great Tudor and Stuart houses

In Tudor times, rich families liked to show how wealthy they were by building very big houses. They were often built in an 'E' or 'H' shape. Rich families liked to have their initials or coat of arms carved in stone on the front of the house. Glass became much cheaper in Tudor times, so rich people liked their houses to have many large windows. Having lots of chimneys was also a sign of wealth.

Builders used local materials to build these houses. Some were built of stone (Hardwick Hall), some of brick (Hampton Court), and some were 'half-timbered' (Speke Hall).

Many more materials were used to decorate inside the houses. Stone and marble were carved to make grand fireplaces, and plaster was used to decorate the ceilings. The walls of many rooms were covered with oak panels and decorated with tapestries.

▲ "Hardwick Hall, more glass than wall." The Tudor mansion, Hardwick Hall, in Derbyshire, was built by Elizabeth, Countess of Shrewsbury. Can you see her initials at the top of the turrets?

◀ Speke Hall, a typical half-timbered Tudor manor house. The spaces in the timber frame were filled with straw and dried mud, called 'wattle and daub'.

▶ The maze at Hampton Court.

◀ **Blenheim Palace in Oxfordshire was designed by a Stuart architect called Vanbrugh.**

Stuart houses

In Stuart times, there was less good timber for building. More houses were built with brick or stone. Tudor landowners often designed their own houses, but in Stuart times more landowners paid architects to design their buildings for them.

Mansions had many rooms with lots of corridors. Some had a long hall called a gallery. The family could walk along the gallery for exercise or to look at its collection of paintings. Each house had a great hall where meals were eaten and guests entertained.

Gardens and games

Great Tudor and Stuart houses were surrounded by beautiful gardens. There were bright flowers, vegetable and herb gardens, and fruit trees. Owners of the largest houses planted mazes of green hedges in their gardens to entertain guests. Around the gardens were parks where deer and hares were hunted.

Inside the big houses games such as chess and backgammon were played. Musicians, acrobats and jugglers came and performed. Great feasts were held with many different kinds of meat. New foods, like potatoes, sugar, melons, tomatoes and turkey, came from the Americas and other distant lands. All this food was cooked and served by the family's servants, who lived in simple rooms in part of the manor house.

Life in the towns

Towns were very crowded, busy and noisy. Markets were held three times a week and fairs twice a year. Before the Great Fire of London (in 1666) there was no town planning. Houses were built very close together. Streets were narrow and dark. Rubbish was simply thrown out onto the street.

There were many different traders in towns. There was usually a cordwainer (shoemaker), a glover (glovemaker), a chandler (candlemaker), a cooper (barrel-maker), and a glazier (glassmaker).

Other goods were made in small factories which sometimes used water mills to work machines. Masters and factory owners trained apprentices for seven years to learn their craft.

Traders often joined together to form a group or 'guild'. Guilds made rules about who could join their trade and how their goods should be sold.

Few people could read so traders had pictures on their signs to show what they were selling.

Rich people sometimes carried bags of herbs and spices called 'pomanders' to stop them smelling the rotting rubbish in the streets.

This is how a typical London street may have looked in Tudor times.

◀ This is a map of London in Tudor times. It is only a short walk from Charing Cross into the country. Today Charing Cross is in the centre of London, many miles from the countryside.

▼ Traders often joined together to form guilds. Members of the guilds met in guildhalls. Guildhalls like this can be seen in many towns today.

Shops were open at the front. Most things were hand-made by skilled craftspeople who worked behind the shops. The streets were often named after the craftspeople or tradespeople who worked there (e.g. Cooper Street).

At night it was easy for thieves to rob people in the dark narrow streets. Some towns made laws to stop anyone going out into the streets after 9 o'clock at night.

Law and order

In English towns laws and rules were made by the mayor, members of the guilds, and other important people. They made laws about how the streets should be cleaned and mended. They paid night watchmen to make sure no one was out after 9 o'clock at night. They made sure shops were closed on Sundays and that fierce dogs were muzzled. They decided how markets and fairs would be run. They also gave money and coal to the poor.

Trade and travel

In Tudor and Stuart times many people grew their own food and wove their own clothes. But they still needed to buy things which they could not make, like spices, tools and weapons. Sometimes they simply exchanged or swapped things. But to buy things at markets, or from travelling pedlars, they needed money.

The Tudor and Stuart rulers ordered money to be made at the Royal Mint. The coins always had a picture of the ruler on them. Oliver Cromwell had his own picture put on coins made when he was in power (see page 19).

Coins showing the heads of Tudor and Stuart monarchs.

James I

Charles I

Henry VIII

Travel by road was slow and uncomfortable. Thieves and highwaymen were common.

Travel by road

Most people stayed close to where they lived and did not travel far. But some people had to travel to sell goods or to visit relatives. 'Post-boys' and 'post-horses' carried letters around the country. During the Civil War armies also had to travel many miles.

The roads that were used had been built by the Romans over a thousand years before. Each town was supposed to look after its own roads and bridges. But often the roads were not cleared or repaired, and bridges were especially dangerous.

In Stuart times coaches became more popular. Companies maintained the roads, but they charged people money to use them. They set up 'turnpikes' along the road, where travellers had to pay 'tolls' to pass.

Travel by waterway

It was often easier and cheaper to send goods by water. Barges and little sailing ships were used to travel along rivers and around the coast. This was the only way to carry fragile loads like pottery or heavy loads such as corn, stone, or 'sea-coal' (coal found in cliffs and on the sea-shore). Most of the big cities could be reached in this way.

▲ Ships could travel up the River Thames to trade in London.

Travel by sea

Passengers could travel on 'packet' ships across the Channel to ports in Europe. English goods like cloth and fish were sold abroad and goods like wine and timber were brought back. But trade across the Channel was dangerous. Captains had to steer their ships through bad weather and past dangerous sandbanks. There was even the risk of being attacked by enemy ships or by pirates.

Rich merchants began to sail their ships across the oceans to explore new lands. They traded with foreign countries and brought back new foods and goods like sugar, spices, silks, furs and timber. But only the rich people of England and Wales could afford to buy them.

Some English people stayed in these foreign countries in trading posts. These trading posts soon grew into small towns that were called 'colonies'.

The loss of the *Mary Rose*

In 1510, Henry VIII ordered a new warship to be built. He named her after Mary Rose, his favourite sister. The ship was fitted with 91 heavy guns.

In 1545 she and other warships left Portsmouth to fight the French Navy. Henry was in Southsea Castle, watching his fleet sail out. The *Mary Rose* had her gun-ports open and guns ready for firing. But there were far too many men on board. A big wave made the tall ship lean over. The heavily-armed soldiers were thrown to one side of the deck. Water rushed into the ship through the open gun-ports. The *Mary Rose* sank before the King's eyes, and 600 sailors were drowned.

Raising the *Mary Rose*

Modern divers have made many visits to the wreck on the sea bed. One of these divers was Margaret Rule. In 1982 she led a team of divers and archaeologists who wanted to raise the *Mary Rose* to the surface.

First the wreck was gently fixed to a steel cradle. Then a lifting crane slowly raised the cradle out of the sea. The ship is now in dry dock at Portsmouth where it has to be sprayed continuously with water to preserve what remains of the very old oak.

▶ In October 1982, the hull of the *Mary Rose* was lifted above the surface of the water where it had lain for over 400 years.

LOOKING AT EVIDENCE

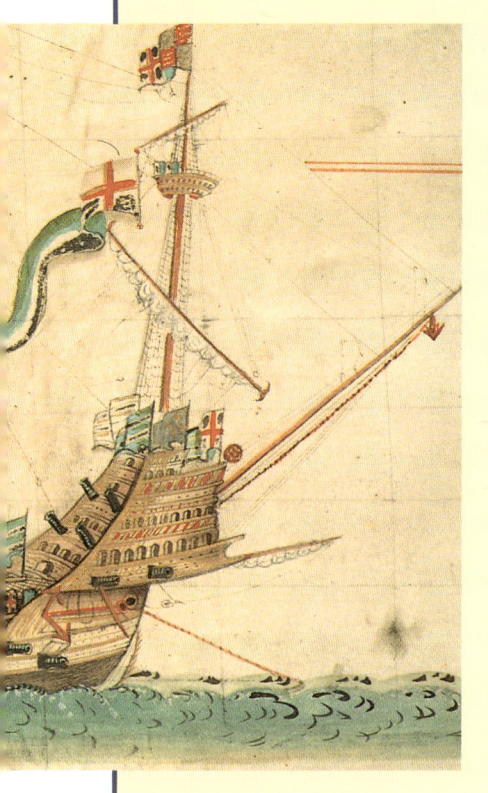

The *Mary Rose* is famous because the remains of the ship tell us a lot about the life Tudor sailors lived at sea. Archaeologists have restored hundreds of items found in the ship. Skeletons of the crew were also found, even the skeleton of a pet dog.

▲ These syringes were amongst the medical equipment found on the *Mary Rose*.

▲ This picture of the *Mary Rose* was painted at the time of Henry VIII.

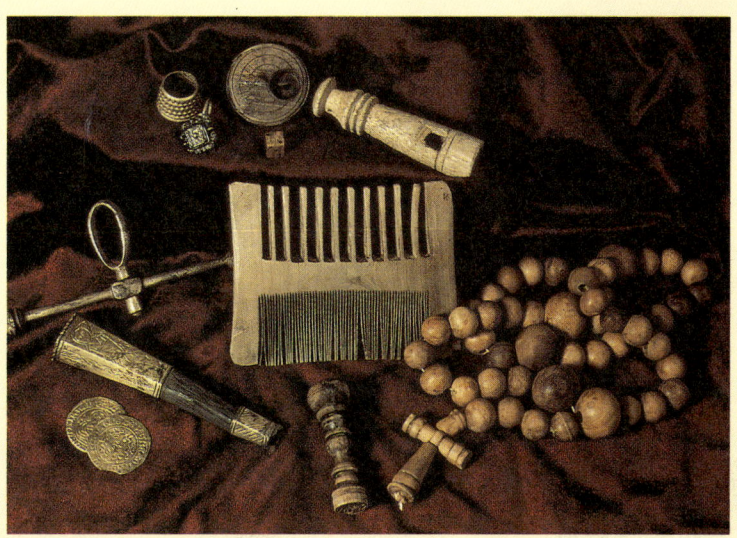

▲ Tudor sailors took board-games onto the ships to help pass long journeys. This backgammon board was recovered from the *Mary Rose*.

◀ These items were found on the *Mary Rose*. They may have belonged to one of the ship's officers.

More objects found on the *Mary Rose* can be seen on page 11 of the *Ginn History Exploration and Encounters* Book.

Shakespeare and the Globe

William Shakespeare was born in 1564 in Henley Street, Stratford-upon-Avon. His family were quite wealthy; his father was a 'whittawer' (a maker of leather gloves and sandles).

At the age of 18 Shakespeare married Anne Hathaway. They had three children. Shakespeare did a number of different jobs, but he really wanted to be an actor and a writer. He began to write poems and plays.

When he was 28 he went to London and joined a group of actors. Soon they began to perform the plays Shakespeare had written. Some of his plays were comedies, which always had happy endings. Some were tragedies, which always had sad endings. Some were plays about the lives of kings, called histories. They became very popular. Even Queen Elizabeth I invited the actors to perform at her court.

In 1603 James I became king of England. He also enjoyed watching the actors perform. He decided that they should be called 'The King's Men'.

Shakespeare became a wealthy man. When he was 46 he returned to Stratford-upon-Avon. He died in 1616, when he was 52.

Shakespeare used words so cleverly and beautifully that many people think he was a genius. Today, his plays are performed all over the world.

◀ **William Shakespeare. We still read and perform Shakespeare's plays today.**

This is how the Globe theatre may have looked outside and inside.

The Globe

Many actors travelled around the country performing plays in the open air. Some theatres were built in London. The most famous of these was the Globe, which was built in Southwark in London. It was a round wooden building with an open roof. People came to the Globe and paid to watch plays. Plays were acted from two o'clock in the afternoon until night. There were no women actors, so the women's parts had to be played by young boys.

Shakespeare was one of the owners of the Globe. Many of his plays were performed there. He must have been very upset when, in 1613, the Globe caught fire during a play and was burnt to the ground.

The flag showed that a play was being performed.

Rich people sat in seats in the galleries.

There was a trap-door in the floor. When evil characters in the plays died they pretended to go through the trap-door to hell.

Poor people stood on the ground. They were called 'groundlings'. They often shouted during the plays and threw food at the actors. Shakespeare teased them by writing about the 'groundlings' in his plays.

Adventurers

Sir Francis Drake

There were many famous sailors during the reign of Queen Elizabeth I. Many young men wanted to go to sea and explore new lands. They wanted to find new trade routes and steal treasure. The most famous English sailor of them all is Sir Francis Drake.

Drake had always wanted to be a sailor. He went to sea when he was 15 and sailed as far as the West Indies. In 1572 he sailed to Central America, which was called 'the New World'. The Spaniards had destroyed the great empire of the Aztecs. Now they were sending Aztec gold and silver back to Spain. Drake stole from the Spaniards and returned home a rich man.

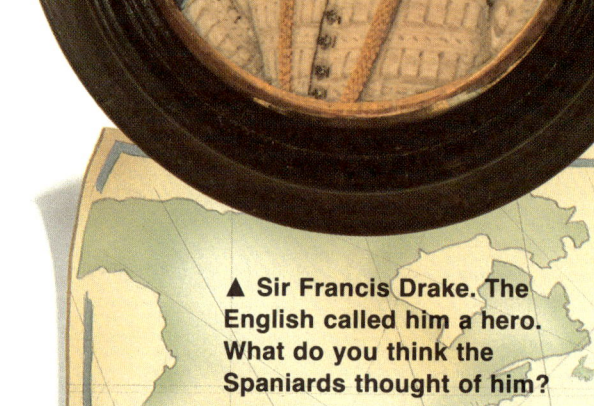

▲ Sir Francis Drake. The English called him a hero. What do you think the Spaniards thought of him?

Drake attacks Spanish ships and steals their gold and silver.

One of Drake's captains, Thomas Doughty, tries to start a mutiny. Drake decides to execute Doughty, but gives him a farewell meal first.

▲ Drake's flagship, the *Golden Hind*.

36

The great adventure

With the money he had stolen from the Spaniards, Drake planned a new adventure. He decided to sail right around the world. On the way he planned to find new trade routes, trade for spices, and steal more gold and silver from the Spaniards.

Drake's journey lasted four years. He attacked many Spanish ships, stealing tons of gold and silver. At that time England and Spain were enemies, but they were not at war. When Drake returned to England he did not know if the Queen would have him executed for attacking the Spaniards and acting like a pirate. But Elizabeth treated him like a hero and made him a knight.

When the Spanish Armada attacked Drake became an even greater hero (see page 10).

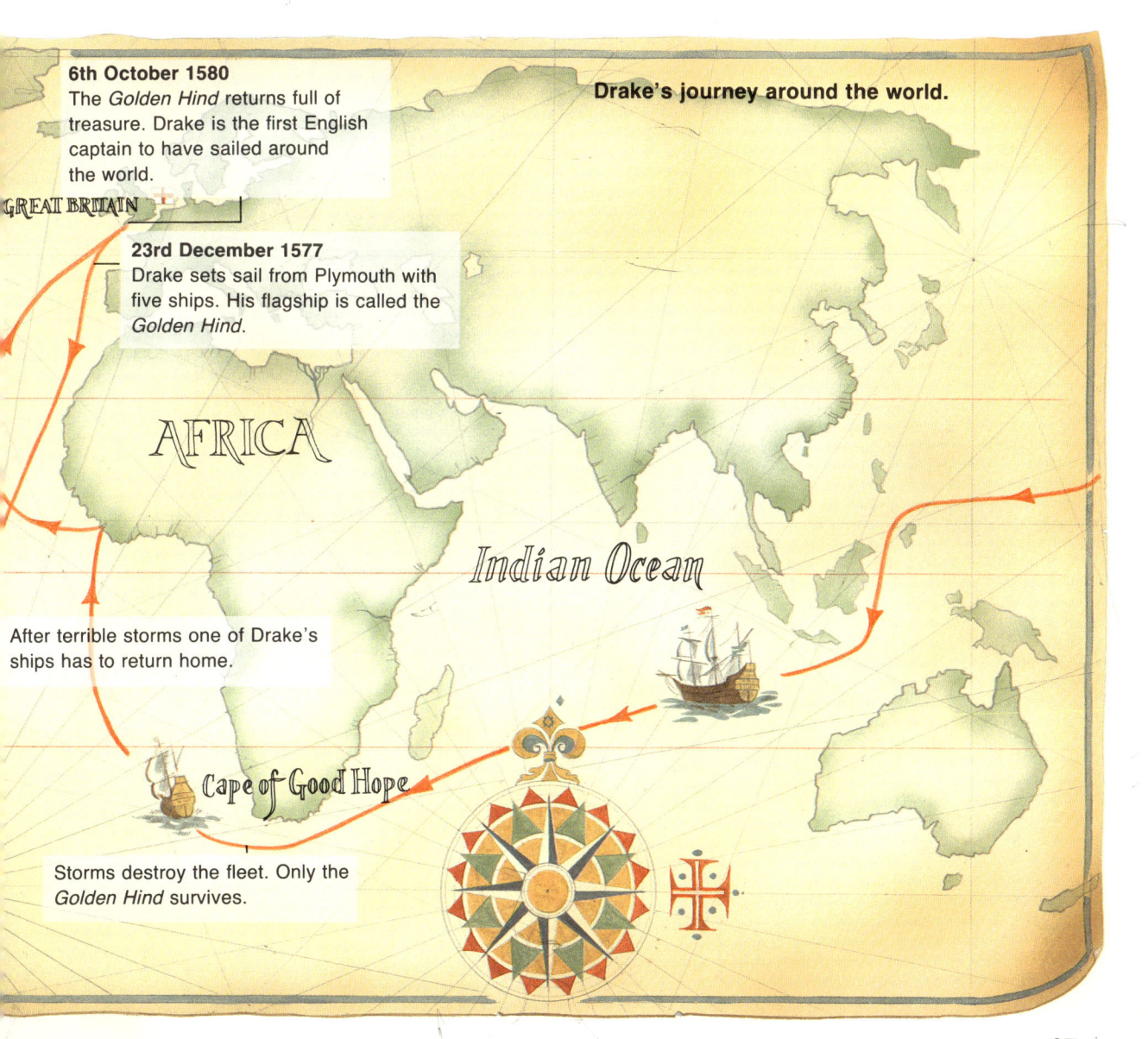

Drake's journey around the world.

6th October 1580
The *Golden Hind* returns full of treasure. Drake is the first English captain to have sailed around the world.

GREAT BRITAIN

23rd December 1577
Drake sets sail from Plymouth with five ships. His flagship is called the *Golden Hind*.

AFRICA

Indian Ocean

After terrible storms one of Drake's ships has to return home.

Cape of Good Hope

Storms destroy the fleet. Only the *Golden Hind* survives.

Adventurers

Sir Walter Raleigh

When Walter Raleigh was a boy he listened to many stories about men who went to sea and had great adventures. He wanted to be an explorer when he grew up.

Raleigh became one of Queen Elizabeth's courtiers. The Queen liked talking to him and asking his advice. Raleigh became the Queen's favourite courtier. She made him a knight and gave him houses and lands.

One story tells how Raleigh put his cloak on the ground so that Queen Elizabeth could walk on the cloak rather than through a puddle.

The American colonies

Raleigh asked the Queen if he could sail to the 'New World' and build new English trading posts called colonies. But the Queen would not allow Raleigh to leave her court. So Raleigh paid sailors to sail to the 'New World' without him. They took families with them who wanted to live in the 'New World'. These families were called colonists. His sailors reached America. They started a colony there and called it Virginia. The sailors brought back potatoes and tobacco, which had never been seen in England before.

The colonists in Virginia did not settle in their new home. Instead of planting crops they spent a lot of their

◀ Portrait of Raleigh.

▶ The Tower of London today. Raleigh was imprisoned here by King James I for 13 years.

time searching for gold and silver. Soon they did not have enough food to eat. After only a year they returned to England.

In 1587 Raleigh sent more colonists to North America. Three years later an English ship went to visit the colony. They found the empty huts of the colonists but no people. No one knows what happened to them.

In Stuart times more colonists went to America and built colonies. The most famous of these were the Puritans who sailed to America on *The Mayflower* in 1620. The Puritans worked hard on their farms and grew enough food to eat. Their descendants still live in America today.

The last adventure

When Queen Elizabeth died, James I became the new king. He did not trust Queen Elizabeth's old advisors. He put Raleigh in prison in the Tower of London. Raleigh stayed there for 13 years. During that time he wrote poems and books and carried out scientific experiments.

Raleigh asked the King if he could be let out of prison and sent on a new expedition. He promised the King that he would sail to South America and find gold. The King let Raleigh sail to South America, but he warned him not to fight the Spaniards. Raleigh could not find any gold. His men attacked a Spanish fort. When Raleigh returned to England he was tried and executed.

Plague!

In Tudor and Stuart times doctors did not know as much about medicine as we do today. They thought that people were ill because they had done something wrong. They believed the only way to cure people was by letting the illness come out of their body, often by cutting them to let blood flow out or by putting leeches on them. These cures did not help the patients, in fact they often killed them!

With no proper medicines it was easy for illnesses to spread from one person to another. Sometimes so many people became ill that the illness became a plague. There had already been plagues in Stuart England, in 1603, 1625 and 1636, but the great plague of 1665 was the worst of them all.

▲ Doctors during the plague sometimes wore protective clothing like this. The nose cone was filled with herbs. These costumes did not stop doctors from catching the illness.

1 Ships trading in the port of London were full of black rats.

2 Fleas lived on the rats. These fleas carried the plague disease. They jumped from the rats onto people. When they bit people, the people caught the plague. The first cases of plague began in June 1665 in London.

Up; and put on my coloured silk suit, very fine, and my new periwigg, bought a good while since but durst not wear because the plague was in Westminster when i bought it; and it is a wonder what will be the fashion after the plague is done as to periwiggs, for nobody will dare to buy any hairs for fear of infection, that it had been cut off the heads of people dead of the plague……..

◀ This is a translation from Samuel Pepys' diary from September 3rd 1665.

How did the plague spread?

The summer of 1665 was very hot. The streets of London were crowded and dirty. It was easy for the plague to spread. Nearly 70,000 Londoners died that year. It continued to spread to other areas of the country until March 1666.

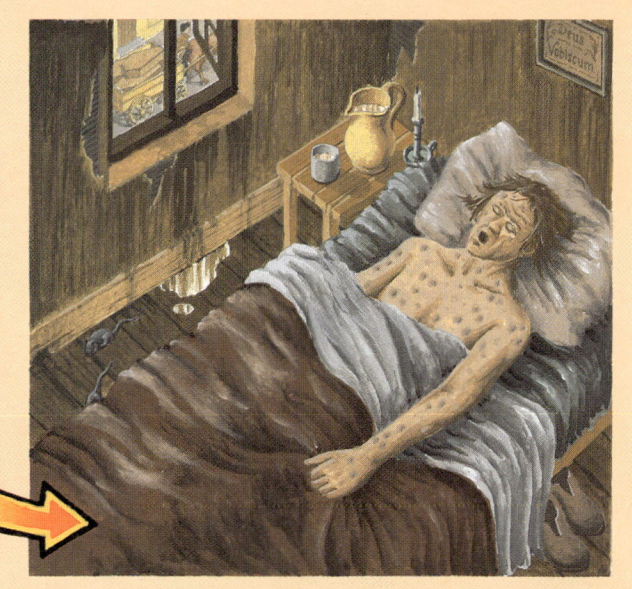

3 People who caught the plague became covered in ugly dark swellings called 'buboes'. (The disease is called bubonic plague.) They either recovered or were dead in a week.

London during the plague

The Lord Mayor of London made new laws to try to stop the plague spreading. A red cross was painted on the door of houses where plague sufferers lived. A notice was also put on the door saying 'Lord have mercy upon us'. Animals were killed to stop them carrying the illness.

Doctors wore special clothes to prevent them from catching the disease. Some doctors pretended that they had a cure for the plague. These 'quack' doctors charged people lots of money for their cure.

The plague killed so many people that the streets, markets and inns became empty. 'Corpse-bearers' pushed carts around the streets collecting dead bodies. The 'corpse-bearers' rang a bell and called out 'Bring out your dead!'.

Rich people left London to stay with friends or relatives in the country. King Charles II moved his court from London to Oxford.

The Great Fire of London

The fire begins

Thomas Farynor was a baker who lived in Pudding Lane in London. On Saturday September 1st, 1666, Farynor thought he had put out his oven fires and went to bed. But one of the ovens was still alight. Soon the whole house was on fire. Farynor and his family jumped from a window to safety. But the wind blew the fire into the stables of the Star Inn nearby. The fire was spreading rapidly!

Samuel Pepys (see page 21) got up that night to see what was happening, but he went back to bed again. Fires were common in London at that time. But this was no ordinary fire.

The fire spread from house to house and then along London Bridge and the bank of the Thames. Most of the houses in London were timber-framed. Many had thatched roofs. They were built very close together. The fire spread easily, blowing down the narrow streets. By midday on Sunday the fire was still spreading. The whole of London was in danger.

1 Farynor left one of his baking ovens alight. His house caught fire and the family had to escape out of a window.

2 Samuel Pepys buried all his most valuable things in his garden. He buried his best wines, important papers about his work in the Navy and, of course, his diary.

Fighting the fire

Many Londoners began to leave the city and escape into the countryside or across the River Thames. They loaded their things onto carts and boats and left their houses to burn. These carts jammed the narrow streets and got in the way of the fire fighters.

◀ Syringes like this were used to fight the Great Fire.

▶ Sir Christopher Wren designed and built 51 new churches. The greatest of them was St Paul's Cathedral.

Soldiers pulled houses down with iron hooks. They even used gunpowder to blow up houses in the path of the fire.

Watchmen and constables tried to put out the fire. They used buckets and syringes filled with water from public wells and fountains. But the summer of 1666 had been very hot and most of the fountains were dry.

The end of the fire

The Lord Mayor of London did not know how to stop the fire. Samuel Pepys went to see King Charles II in his London palace to ask for help to stop the Great Fire.

Charles II ordered houses in the path of the fire to be pulled down. He sent soldiers to help the fire fighters. But the fire continued to spread. Finally, on Wednesday September 5th, the wind changed direction and the fire stopped spreading.

The fire had spread for four days. Most of London had been destroyed. 86 churches and 13,000 houses had been burnt down. Even St Paul's Cathedral was gone. Thousands of people had nowhere to live. The King ordered tents to be put up for the homeless and that the water and rubbish be cleared from the streets. London had to be rebuilt.

A new London

Great architects like Christopher Wren helped to plan the new city. They did not want another Great Fire so they decided not to build any more timber-framed houses. Most of the new buildings were built of brick or stone.

They also wanted to build streets that were much wider to stop any new fires spreading. But this would have cost a lot of money. Only a few new wide streets were built. Most new buildings were built where the old ones had stood.

Science

People in Tudor and Stuart times wanted to learn more about science. Some read books written by the Ancient Greek and Roman scientists over 1,000 years ago. But others thought that the Ancient Greeks and Romans might not always be correct. They had new ideas about how the earth, the universe, and living things worked. These scientists began to do experiments to see if their ideas were correct.

How does the heart work?

Dr William Harvey was a medical scientist who had a new idea about how our heart and lungs work. No one understood why the heart beats or what the pulse is. Harvey thought that the heart was a pump that sent blood out through the arteries and back through the veins. On the way the blood passed through the lungs where it picked up oxygen. By careful experiments and observations he proved he was right.

Finding the way

When ships sail out of sight of land the captain has to work out which direction to steer the ship in. This is called navigation. During Tudor and Stuart times many ships sailed across the oceans looking for new trade routes and lands. New instruments were made to help ships' captains navigate. (You can find out more about navigation instruments on page 12 of the *Ginn History Exploration and Encounters Book*.)

Looking at the stars

New navigational instruments were also used to look at the stars. The craftspeople who made these instruments also learnt how to make telescopes and microscopes.

◀ A 17th century microscope.

Sir Isaac Newton

Sir Isaac Newton used these new telescopes to look at the stars. He worked out how the moon moves round the earth, and how the earth and other planets move round the sun. He realised that there must be a force making the planets pull at one another. He called this force gravity. At the time many people laughed at Newton's ideas, but today we know this force exists and we call it gravity.

Newton also made many new discoveries about mathematics and light. Many people think that Newton was a genius, one of the cleverest people who has ever lived.

One story tells how Newton first had his idea about gravity when an apple fell from a tree and hit him on the head.

To myself I seem to have been like a boy playing on the seashore and now and then finding a smoother pebble or a prettier shell than ordinary, while the great ocean Truth lay undiscovered before me.

This is what Newton said about his own investigations.

The Royal Society

King Charles II was very interested in new ideas. He founded the Royal Society to bring scientists together to share ideas. Many scientists joined the society, including Isaac Newton and Sir Christopher Wren. The Royal Society still exists today.

Religion and Superstition

The King James Bible

Before Tudor times most copies of the Bible were still written in Latin, which only a few people could read.
Henry VIII ordered the Bible to be written in English and put in every church. When James I became king he ordered a better translation to be made.

A group of experts translated the Bible from Latin into English. It took them many years. This new translation of the Bible was printed on slow printing presses. In 1611 the new King James Bible was finished.

▶ King James I.

Most copies went to churches to be read out to the people. Some rich people bought their own copies. Soon the King James Bible became very popular. Many people still use the King James translation today.

◀ Oliver Cromwell's copy of the King James Bible.

▼ 17th century picture of a witch being thrown into a pond.

Witches

In Tudor and Stuart times many people believed in witches. Even King James I believed in witches and wrote a book about them. Today we call this 'superstition'. Superstition means believing in something that is unknown or mysterious.

In Tudor and Stuart times if someone became ill or if their crops failed to grow they wanted to blame someone. They thought that a witch must have cast an evil spell on them. And so they went looking for witches. Usually they picked on old women because they thought that if someone lived for a very long time it was because they had magic powers.

These poor old women were put on trial and often tortured and killed. Many were tied up and thrown into ponds. If they floated they were thought to be guilty of witchcraft and were hanged. If they sank they were thought to be innocent, but by the time they were pulled out they were often dead anyway.

47

Glossary

These words are underlined in this book.

Ambassadors
Important people sent by one country to another as representatives. Sometimes ambassadors carry special messages.

Annul
To take away the meaning of an agreement (like marriage), so that it is as if the agreement was never made.

Apprentices
Young boys and girls who studied a skill or craft with a master craftsperson for a certain number of years.

Bankrupt
A person or an institution with no more money is said to be bankrupt.

Civil war
A war in which members of one country hold different views and fight against one another. There is only one country involved.

Clergy
People who are employed to perform services in Christian churches.

Courtiers
Members of a king's or queen's court.

Descendants
Your descendants are your children and their children's children.

Found(ed)
To set up an institution so that it will last forever.

Genius
A person who is very intelligent.

Jousting
A sport in which knights on horseback fight mock battles with one another.

Monarch
A king or queen.

Muskets
16th century handguns for soldiers.

Pikes
Weapons with long wooden handles and pointed iron heads.

Plot(ted)
To make secret plans.

Puritans
People who thought that religious rules should be stricter, and that one should dress and live as simply as possible.

Rebellion
An open and organised fight against a ruler or a government.

Scholars
Serious students or pupils.

Taxes/taxed
Payments of money or services to the government.

Thresh(ed)
To separate the grain or seeds from a plant by beating it.

Treason
Disloyalty to one's country or government.

Tried
When someone is tried, their guilt or innocence is examined in a court of law.